MW00884606

Modeling
The Master

Effective Use of Metaphor in Christian Counseling

By

Larry W. Bailey, PhD.

Clinical Psychologist

Modeling The Master
by Larry W. Bailey, PhD.

Printed in the United States of America

ISBN 1-591609-28-3

Xulon Press
www.XulonPress.com

Xulon Press books are available in bookstores everywhere, and on the Web at www.XulonPress.com.

Contents

꩜꩜

Preface

In a recent article in the *Journal of Psychology and Christianity,* Kamila Blessing (2002) draws several parallels between Jesus' use of parables and Milton Erickson's use of metaphor to bring about positive change in those who would hear. Both men were very effective in influencing others through the use of stories which convey a needed thought in a way that would engage the listener, bypass resistance, and allow the hearer to participate in the interpretation and application of the message. Blessing's focus was rather limited due to the format, but she concluded that there is need for further development of the use of parables as a tool for therapy and pastoral counseling (p. 167). Such development is the purpose of this book. I have been exploring the parallels between the teachings of Jesus and the therapeutic methods of Erickson for two years, seeking to integrate and organize the learning in order to share helpful concepts with other Christian counselors.

This book has five main sections. In chapter one we review the counseling literature that relates to using metaphor to both understand and influence counselees. Attention is then given to the use of indirect, metaphoric communication in Scripture, especially in Jesus' use of parables (chapter two). Insights gained from counseling literature and the gospels are integrated in order to understand the use of metaphor in contemporary Christian counseling. There are several basic principles which facilitate the formulation and delivery of stories with therapeutic intent (chapter three), and inform the use of activities designed to positively influence counselees (chapter four). Practical issues in the use of metaphor are addressed in chapter five.

I have greatly benefited from the encouraging support and input from my wife, Anita Bailey; Gillian Heine; Steven Ware; and Tracy Michaels. I hope that the material presented in this book is a blessing to those who engage in the intriguing ministry of Christian counseling.

Introduction

*M*any years ago in a dusty village of a distant land, a boy grew up in a carpenter's home. He matured into a very observant young man, noting well the processes of nature and the activities of people in his community. He came to understand the necessity of proper planning in the family business; the routines and challenges of the farmers, shepherds and fishermen; the workings of the marketplace; the principles and practices of religion; and social customs and concerns.

Sensitivity to his surroundings greatly enhanced this man's later efforts to encourage people to make significant changes. He wanted to help people change from old ways of thinking to new patterns of thought; discover an appropriate concept of self; find a more joyful, abundant life; reduce anxiety and discouragements; re-evaluate priorities; develop more meaningful relationships; and establish a fresh and fulfilling relationship with God.

In his attempts to bring about pervasive changes in the lives of people, the man frequently used a metaphorical approach – parables, similes, and analogies. His stories and figures of speech attest to his astute awareness of the everyday events of his world. His effectiveness in such communication is evident as his detractors call him "Rabbi," and educators refer to him as the Master Teacher.

Throughout the history of psychotherapy there has been an appreciation of the reality of multilevel communication. Theorists such as Sigmund Freud, Carl Jung, Eric Berne and Milton Erickson have understood that much of our discourse involves more than the overtly stated words. Freud spoke of the role of unconscious factors in determining hidden meanings of verbalizations, Jung was intrigued by the symbolism represented in communication patterns, and Berne noted that discourse includes both social and psychological meanings. Erickson became well known for his keen sensitivity to the role of metaphors and parallel communication in the conversation of a wide variety of patients (e.g., schizophrenics who "live in a metaphorical world," neurotics, married couples).

For those of a classic psychoanalytic orientation, the significance of multilevel communication has been addressed primarily as a means of identifying the underlying conflicts and motivational issues of the patient. The therapist would be attentive to speech patterns, blocks and digressions associated with critical topics, and the symbolic meaning of dreams. The material obtained from these and other sources would be used therapeutically to facilitate interpretations, deal with conflicted feelings, and develop insight (Siegelman, 1990).

More recent advancements in the field of psychotherapy include serious consideration of ways in which multilevel communication may be used by the therapist to influence the thoughts and behavior of the client. Milton Erickson and his students/colleagues have been the predominant figures in demonstrating the positive therapeutic impact of stories, analogies and other types of parallel communication (Gafner & Benson, 2003; Gilligan, 1990; Haley, 1973; Lankton, 1990; Madanes, 1990; O'Hanlon, 1987; Rosen, 1982; Rossi & Ryan, 1985; Simpkins & Simpkins, 2001; Thompson, 1990; Zeig, 1975; Zeig & Geary, 2000;). Others who have made significant contributions to understanding the use of metaphors in therapy include Barker (1985, 1996), Gordon (1978), Ingram (1996), Kopp (1971), and Voth (1970). Multilevel communication is seen as crucial for both *understanding* the framework and feelings of the counselee, and therapeutic *intervention.*

The purpose of this book is to consider the rationale and techniques of indirect communication typical of Ericksonian therapies, and extend the principles to a Christian counseling approach that incorporates the wisdom of Biblical metaphor (especially parables and similes).

Chapter 1

Indirect Communication in Counseling

Several approaches to therapy place a high value on the role of indirect or multilevel communication in understanding and/or influencing counselees. Therapists give serious consideration to the poignant stories, metaphors (figurative language), analogies and similes (comparison of two dissimilar things) conveyed by both counselee and counselor. Such communication often contains "hidden messages" or "subtle feelings" which are significant to the therapeutic process.

Understanding the Counselee

Careful attention to the indirect communication of a counselee helps the counselor to enter his/her frame of reference and develop empathic understanding. The observant therapist is responsive to perspectives, emotional tone, implicit expectations and suggested outcomes conveyed in the client's metaphors. For example, I am working with a young woman who was rejected by her lover. She reports, "When he left, I felt like a crushed peanut!" Her expansion on the metaphor included the ideas of "being in many pieces" and feeling "belittled." The imagery, direction of movement and affect are much different than that which may have been expressed as having been "blown away" or "wiped out."

Two examples from the counseling literature are helpful in further appreciating the role of metaphor in understanding the counselee.

> In a case where a boy was reported to be afraid of dogs, the therapist learned that the boy had been adopted as an infant. The boy ostensibly did not know he had been adopted, and the parents did not wish to tell him. The therapist assumed the boy did know. The therapist wanted to get the family to take a dog into the home and also wanted to deal with the adoption issue. Therefore, he talked to the boy about "adopting" a dog who had a problem of being frightened. He then discussed with the boy various issues, such as the possibility that the dog might become ill and have to be taken to the doctor (which situation paralleled the adopted boy being taken to the doctor). When the boy said the family might have to get rid of the dog if he became ill and cost doctor bills, the therapist insisted that once adopted the family was committed to the dog and would have to keep him and pay his doctor bills no matter what. Various concerns the boy might have had about himself as well as the parents' concerns about him were discussed in metaphoric terms in relation to the proposed adoption of the puppy.
>
> (Haley, 1976, p.65)
>
> When Erickson was on the staff of Worcester State Hospital, there was a young patient who called himself Jesus. He paraded about as the Messiah, wore a sheet draped around him, and attempted to impose Christianity on people. Erickson approached him on the hospital grounds and said, "I understand you have had experience as a carpenter?" The patient could only reply that he had. Erickson involved the young man in a special project of building a bookcase and shifted him to productive labor.
>
> (Haley, 1973, p.28)

A broad range of therapists grasp the importance of understanding thoughts and feelings couched in metaphorical language. The psychoanalyst attends to the indirect expressions of the effects of early experience and of dream images (Ingram, 1996; Siegelman, 1990; Voth, 1970); the family therapist is attuned to material pertaining to issues of control, priorities, love and forgiveness (Combs and Freedman, 1990; Madanes, 1990); those of an Ericksonian orientation listen for clues to the counselee's frame of reference, values, interests and strengths (Gilligan, 1990; Haley, 1973; Lankton, 1990; O'Hanlon, 1987; Zeig, 1985); the cognitive therapist seeks to determine core themes and irrational beliefs which may be conveyed indirectly (McMullen, 2000); and a relational counseling approach includes listening for sensory images used by the helpee (e.g., "I see ... hear ... feel ...") so that the helper may match the helping language to the counselee's dominant sensory mode (Brammer and MacDonald, 1999). A counselor must be attentive to the counselee's metaphoric language in order to develop a therapeutic understanding of the person being helped.

Influencing the Counselee

One of the unique features of the strategic, brief-therapy approaches associated with Erickson and his colleagues is the attention given to the use of metaphor in therapeutic intervention. It is assumed that the counselee has untapped growth potential, unrecognized capability, and motivation for change. The therapist, having developed an understanding of the issues and interests being communicated by the client, may formulate and deliver a metaphorical message with the goal of influencing the counselee at the cognitive, emotional and/or behavioral level. Such indirect, multilevel communication (usually presented without interpretation) has been found to be effective for suggesting new ideas (Combs and Freedman, 1990; Gafner and Benson, 2003; Haley, 1973; O'Hanlon, 1987; Zeig, 1985), stimulating new associations (Ingram, 1996; Sigelman, 1990; Victor, 1977), modifying one's perception of the past (Thompson, 1990), developing an openness to alternative coping strategies (Combs and Freedman, 1990; O'Hanlon, 1987; Thompson, 1990), reframing

(Combs and Freedman, 1990; Thompson, 1990), and evoking abilities (Combs and Freedman, 1990; O'Hanlon, 1987; Zeig, 1985). Some examples of using parallel communication to influence the counselee toward growth follow.

> A 12-year-old boy was brought to Erickson for bedwetting. Erickson dismissed his parents and immediately began talking to the boy about other topics, avoiding a discussion of bedwetting altogether. Upon learning that the boy played baseball and his brother football, Erickson began to describe the fine muscle coordination it takes to play baseball compared to the gross, uncoordinated muscle skills used in football. The boy listened raptly as Erickson described in some detail all the fine muscle adjustments his body made automatically in order to position him underneath the ball and to catch it. The glove has to be opened up just at the right moment and clamp down again just at the right moment. When transferring the ball to another hand, the same kind of fine muscle control was needed. Then, when throwing the ball to the infield, if one lets go of it too soon, it doesn't go where one wants it to go. Likewise, letting go too late leads to frustration. Letting go just at the right time gets it to go where one wants it to go, and that constitutes success … in baseball.
>
> (O'Hanlon, 1987, p. 74)

If Erickson is dealing with a married couple that has a conflict over sexual relations and would rather not discuss it directly, he will approach the problem metaphorically. He will choose some aspect of their lives that is analogous to sexual relations and change that as a way of changing the sexual behavior. He might, for example, talk to them about having dinner together and draw them out on their preferences. He will discuss with them how the wife likes appetizers before dinner, while the husband prefers to dive right into the meat and potatoes.

Or the wife might prefer a quiet and leisurely dinner, while the husband, who is quick and direct, just wants the meal over with. If the couple begins to connect what they are saying with sexual relations, Erickson will "drift rapidly" away to other topics, and then he will return to the analogy. He might end such a conversation with a directive that the couple arrange a pleasant dinner for a particular evening that is satisfactory to both of them. When successful, this approach shifts that couple from a more pleasant dinner to more pleasant sexual relations without their being aware that he has deliberately set this goal.

(Haley, 1973, p.27)

A male patient who had had a traumatic series of childhood losses: the death of an uncle when the patient was five, the death of his father when he was eight, and death of his grandfather (his father-surrogate) when the patient turned 18. Apparently, any loss could feed into this man's long-defended-against grieving and experience of dependency. At one period in the treatment, the patient had had some of his clothes stolen from a laundry; he was both outraged and impelled to replace the lost items immediately (a response that reflected his typical way of dealing with loss). He speculated about getting someone to help him with this problem. Knowing that the patient's father had been a tailor, the analyst made the following comment:

I suggested that he needed a tailor and asked him if he knew of any way to mend the situation. This ambiguous metaphor was a reference to his major loss in childhood ... his recent loss ... and to myself in the transference as one who mends or helps him mend himself. He recalled with vivid details for the first time a particular garment his father had made for him, just before his terminal illness. He remembered his giving it to him; and with affect he continued with new details of the later loss of the grandfather.

The metaphor had brought the good father into the present in the transference. Shortly after remembering and working through this material, the patient, who had been psychologically paralyzed for months, was able to look for and find a job.

(Siegelman, 1990, p.104)

The diversity of cases represented in the examples cited demonstrates the wide range of situations in which metaphorical intervention may be utilized. In each instance, the therapist was keenly aware of the concerns and interests of the counselee, translated across modalities, and communicated a deeply meaningful story. Thompson has suggested that the use of metaphor to influence the counselee is "a method to let the truth be learned by appearing to not teach" (1990, p.247).

Chapter 2

Indirect Communication in Scripture

The use of metaphor to instruct, influence, comfort and confront is found throughout Scripture. Indeed, very early in human history God the Creator used a metaphoric approach in dealing with the first murderer, Cain. He said, "What have you done? The voice of your brother's blood is crying to me from the ground!" (Genesis 4:10). Magnificent word pictures are used in psalms, proverbs, prophecies, gospels and epistles to describe God and His people. Among the more psychologically notable depictions of God include His role as protective shield (Psalms. 3:3, 18:2, 28:7), secure stronghold for those who are troubled and distressed (Psalms 9:9, 18:2, 27:1; Isaiah 25:4), safe refuge in times of difficulty (2 Samuel 22:3, Psalms 31:2, Jeremiah 16:19), nurturing shepherd that comforts and guides (Psalms 23, Is. 40:11), and strong tower (Proverbs 18:10). His human-like attributes include supportive hands for those afflicted (Psalms 10:14, 18:35), a listening ear for the fatherless and oppressed (Psalms 10:18), a watchful eye upon his people (Psalms 33:18), a mouth that speaks truthfully (Psalms 119:72, Isaiah1:20, 40:5), and strong arms (Psalms 44:3, 89:10-13, 91:1). God's people are described as flourishing and fruitful trees (Psalms 1:3, 92:12-14), well attended sheep whose needs are met (Psalms 23, John 10: 1-18), salt of the earth

(Matthew 5:13), light of the world (Matthew 5:14-16), living branches connected to the eternal Vine (John 15: 1-8), members of the body of Christ (Romans 12:5, 1 Corinthians 12:27), children of God (Matthew 7:11, 18:3-4; Ephesians 5:1), and a holy temple (1 Corinthians 3:16-17; 2 Corinthians 6:16). Such metaphors for God and His people have clear implications for the counseling situation in which counselees often experience feelings of inferiority, loneliness, hopelessness, inefficacy and/or vulnerability. Goals in Christian counseling often include moving toward improved "connecting" with God and others, increased growth, more abundant living and a greater sense of self worth and efficacy.

Old Testament Stories to Convey a Message

Several stories in the Old Testament are clearly meant to convey an important message through reference to familiar physical events. Following are two of the more familiar stories used to confront shameful behavior.

> After David had sinned against God by committing adultery with Bathsheba and then arranging for the death of her husband, the Lord sent Nathan to David. Nathan said, "There were two men in a certain town, one rich and the other poor. The rich man had a very large number of sheep and cattle, but the poor man had nothing except one little ewe lamb he had bought. He raised it, and it grew up with him and his children. It shared his food, drank from his cup and even slept in his arms. It was like a daughter to him. Now a traveler came to the rich man, but the rich man refrained from taking one of his own sheep or cattle to prepare a meal for the traveler who had come to him. Instead, he took the ewe lamb that belonged to the poor man and prepared it for the one who had come to him." David burned with anger against the man and said to Nathan, "As surely as the Lord lives, the man who did this deserves to die! He must pay for that lamb four times

over, because he did such a thing and had no pity." Then Nathan said to David, "You are the man!".

(II Samuel 12:1-7)

Following the death of Jerubbaal (Gideon), Abimelech tricked the people and murdered the rightful heirs (except for one – Jotham) in order to become king. When the people gathered beside the great tree at the pillar of Shechem to crown Abimelech king, Jotham climbed a nearby mountain and shouted to them, "Listen to me, citizens of Shechem, so that God may listen to you. One day the trees went out to anoint a king for themselves. They said to the olive tree, 'Be our king.' But the olive tree answered, 'Should I give up my oil, by which both gods and men are honored, to hold sway over the trees?' Next, the trees said to the fig tree, 'Come and be our king.' But the fig tree replied, 'Should I give up my fruit, so good and sweet, to hold sway over the trees?' Then the trees said to the vine, 'Come and be our king." But the vine answered, 'Should I give up my wine, which cheers both gods and men, to hold sway over the trees?' Finally all the trees said to the thorn bush, 'Come and be our king.' The thorn bush said to the trees, 'If you really want to anoint me king over you, come and take refuge in my shade; but if not, then let fire come out of the thorn bush and consume the cedars of Lebanon!' Now if you have acted honorably and in good faith when you made Abimelech king, and if you have been fair to Jerubbaal and his family, and if you have treated him as he deserves … if then you have acted honorably and in good faith toward Jerubbaal and his family today, may Abimelech be your joy, and may you be his, too! But if you have not, let fire come out from Abimelech and consume you, citizens of Shechem and Beth Millo, and consume Abimelech!" Then Jotham fled, escaping to Beer, and he lived there because he was afraid of his brother, Abimelech.

(Judges 9: 8-15)

Another story in the Old Testament is remarkable for its multilevel communication. It conveys messages relating to the task and frustrations in the ministry of Zechariah, the rejection of God by is own people, a symbolic breaking of the covenant, the lost brotherhood between Judah and Israel, and a prophetic allusion to the betrayer of Jesus.

> This is what the Lord my God says: "Pasture the flock marked for slaughter. Their buyers slaughter them and go unpunished. Those who sell them say, 'Praise the Lord, I am rich!' Their own shepherds do not spare them. For I will no longer have pity on the people of the land," declares the Lord. "I will hand everyone over to his neighbor and his king. They will oppress the land, and I will not rescue them from their hands." So I pastured the flock marked for slaughter, particularly the oppressed of the flock. Then I took two staffs and called one Favor and the other Union, and I pastured the flock. In one month I got rid of the three shepherds. The flock detested me, and I grew weary of them and said, "I will not be your shepherd. Let the dying die, and the perishing perish. Let those who are left eat one another's flesh." Then I took my staff called Favor and broke it, revoking the covenant I had made with all nations. It was revoked on that day, and so the afflicted of the flock who were watching me knew it was the word of the Lord. I told them, "If you think it best, give me my pay; but if not, keep it." So they paid me thirty pieces of silver. And the Lord said to me, "Throw it to the potter" – the handsome price at which they priced me! So I took the thirty pieces of silver and threw them into the house of the Lord to the potter. Then I broke my second staff called Union, breaking the brotherhood between Judah and Israel.
>
> (Zechariah 11:4-14)

Of course, there are many additional stories in the Old Testament that were offered or later interpreted as metaphors. Of particular interest to the Christian counselor is the story of Jeremiah's linen belt that illustrates the related problems of pride and inattention to God's ways.

> The Lord said to me: "Go and buy a linen belt and put it around your waist, but do not let it touch water." So I bought a belt, as the Lord directed, and put it around my waist. Then the word of the Lord came to me a second time: "Take the belt you bought and are wearing around your waist, and go now to Perath and hide it there in a crevice in the rocks." So I went and hid it at Perath, as the Lord told me. Many days later the Lord said to me, "Go now to Perath and get the belt I told you to hide there." So I went to Perath and dug up the belt and took it from the place where I had hidden it, but now it was ruined and completely useless. Then the word of the Lord came to me: "This is what the Lord says: 'In the same way I will ruin the pride of Judah and the great pride of Jerusalem. These wicked people, who refuse to listen to my words, who follow the stubbornness of their hearts and go after other gods to serve and worship them, will be like this belt – completely useless! For as a belt is bound around a man's waist, so I bound the whole house of Israel and the whole house of Judah to me,' declares the Lord, 'to be my people for my renown and praise and honor. But they have not listened.'"
>
> (Jeremiah 13:1-11)

A thorough review of Old Testament stories is well beyond the scope of this book, but some learning may be drawn from the examples that have been cited. The stories are **linked to the context** (e.g., the people were gathered at the "great tree" when Jotham told of the process to identify the "king tree"); **dramatic**, using colorful language and surprising candor; and **designed to influence** the feelings and behavior of the hearer(s).

Jesus' Use of Indirect Communication

The teachings of Jesus were intended to invite people to an entirely new relationship with God and with one another. As He sought to influence people to make radical changes in attitudes and behavior (much like the goals of Christian counseling), He often utilized indirect approaches such as parallel communication, analogies, similes and parables.

On several occasions, Jesus used the method of parallel communication. An intriguing example of this approach is when Jesus spoke in the synagogue of His hometown. Note how the listeners were significantly affected (shifting from attentive/affirming/responsive to angry/rejecting/abusive), having understood the "spin" Jesus put on two familiar stories.

> Then He rolled up the scroll, gave it back to the attendant and sat down. The eyes of the synagogue were fastened on Him, and He began by saying to them, "Today this scripture is fulfilled in your hearing." All spoke well of Him and were amazed at the gracious words that came from His lips. "Isn't this Joseph's son?" they asked. Jesus said to them, "Surely you will quote this proverb to me: 'Physician, heal yourself! Do here in your hometown what we have heard that you did in Capernaum.'" "I tell you the truth," he continued, "no prophet is accepted in his hometown." I assure you that there were many widows in Israel in Elijah's time, when the sky was shut for three and a half years and there was a severe famine throughout the land. Yet Elijah was not sent to any of them, but to a widow in Zarephath in the region of Sidon. And there were many in Israel with leprosy in the time of Elisha the prophet, yet not one of them was cleansed – only Naaman the Syrian." All the people in the synagogue were furious when they heard this. They got up, drove Him out of town, and took him to the brow of the hill on which the town was built, in order to throw Him down the cliff. But He walked right

through the crowd and went on His way.

(Luke. 4:20-30)

Other examples of parallel communication include Jesus' response to the disciples of John the Baptist when they ask if he is the Messiah (Matthew 11:2-6); messages delivered to religious leaders and teachers while "speaking to His disciples" (e.g. Luke 20:45-47); and Jesus' comment to Peter while washing the disciples' feet:

"A person who has had a bath needs only to wash his feet; his whole body is clean. And you are clean *physically,* though not every one of you *spiritually.*" For He knew who was going to betray him, and that is why he said not everyone was clean.

(John 13:10-11)

Note a particularly intriguing interaction between Jesus and a "foreign" woman who *joined* the parallel communication and influenced Jesus.

A Canaanite woman from that vicinity came to him, crying out, "Lord, Son of David, have mercy on me! My daughter is suffering terribly from demon-possession," Jesus did not answer a word. So his disciples came to him and urged him. "Send her away, for she keeps crying out after us." He answered, "I was sent only to the lost sheep of Israel." The woman came and knelt before him. "Lord, help me!' she said. He replied, "It is not right to take the children's bread and toss it to the dogs." "Yes, Lord," she said, "but even the dogs eat the crumbs that fall from their masters' table." Then Jesus answered, "Woman, you have great faith! Your request is granted." And her daughter was healed from that very hour.

(Matthew 15:22-28)

Jesus' masterful use of parables is legendary among non-believers as well as believers. A large portion of His teaching involved the use of "earthly stories with a heavenly meaning." His parables were **empathic** (sensing "where the hearers are" physically and psychologically), **earthy** (using images relating to everyday life), **efficient** (relatively brief, conveying a simple message) and **engaging** (employing the element of surprise, exaggeration or role-reversal). The **ending** often had a unique "twist" or an unsettling question.

Of course, most of the parables Jesus told were intended to introduce people to the new Kingdom, and shift their attitudes and actions from law-abiding to grace abiding. However, we therapists readily understand the similarities between coming into a new era of faith and engaging in Christian counseling: A break with a burdensome past, self-examination, development of a new sense of identity, issues of forgiveness, a change of views toward God and others, movement away from resistance and rationalization, new ways of thinking and restoring broken relationships. To the extent that we appreciate these similarities of themes, the parables of the gospels have noteworthy relevance.

Here are some examples of parables that depict issues faced by Christian counselors.

> *Prodigal son.* "There was a man who had two sons. The younger one said to his father, 'Father, give me my share of the estate.' So he divided his property between them. Not long after that, the younger son got together all he had, set off for a distant country and there squandered his wealth in wild living. After he had spent everything, there was a severe famine in that whole country, and he began to be in need. So he went and hired himself out to a citizen of that country, who sent him to his fields to feed pigs. He longed to fill his stomach with the pods that the pigs were eating, but no one gave him anything. When he came to his senses, he said, 'How many of my father's hired men have food to spare, and here I am starving to death! I will set out and go back to my father and say to him: Father, I have sinned against heaven and against you. I am no longer worthy to be called your son; make

me like one of your hired men.' So he got up and went to his father. But while he was still a long way off, his father saw him and was filled with compassion for him; he ran to his son, threw his arms around him and kissed him. The son said to him, 'Father, I have sinned against heaven and against you. I am no longer worthy to be called your son.' But the father said to his servants, 'Quick! Bring the best robe and put it on him. Put a ring on his finger and sandals on his feet. Bring the fattened calf and kill it. Let's have a feast and celebrate. For this son of mine was dead and is alive again; he was lost and is found.' So they began to celebrate. Meanwhile, the older son was in the field. When he came near the house, he heard music and dancing. So he called one of the servants and asked him what was going on. 'Your brother has come,' he replied, 'and your father has killed the fattened calf because he has him back safe and sound.'

"The older brother became angry and refused to go in. So his father went out and pleaded with him. But he answered his father 'Look! All these years I've been slaving for you and never disobeyed your orders. Yet you never gave me even a young goat so I could celebrate with my friends. But when this son of yours who has squandered your property with prostitutes comes home, you kill the fattened calf for him!' 'My son,' the father said, 'you are always with me, and everything I have is yours. But we had to celebrate and be glad, because this brother of yours was dead and is alive again; he was lost and is found.'"

(Luke 15:11-32)

A young man wants to do his own thing, makes poor choices, feels worthless and ashamed, comes to his senses, seeks forgiveness and restoration, is reconciled with his father, experiences a resentful brother.

A father loses his son, waits patiently and hopefully, enthusiastically welcomes and forgives a wayward son, pleads with his other son to have family reconciliation.

A jealous brother experiences anger and says "poor me," resists forgiving, refuses to participate in a family celebration.

> *Great Banquet.* A certain man was preparing a great banquet and invited many guests. At the time of the banquet he sent his servant to tell those who has been invited 'Come, for everything is now ready.' But they all alike began to make excuses. The first said, 'I have just bought a field, and I must go and see it. Please excuse me.' Another said, 'I have just bought five yoke of oxen, and I'm on my way to try them out. Please excuse me.' Still another said, 'I just got married, so I can't come.' The servant came back and reported this to his master. Then the owner of the house became angry and ordered his servant, 'Go out quickly into the streets and alleys of the town and bring in the poor, the crippled, the blind and the lame.'
>
> 'Sir,' the servant said, 'what you ordered has been done, but there is still room.' Then the master told his servant, 'Go out to the roads and country lanes and make them come in, so that my house will be full. I tell you, not one of those men who were invited will get a taste of my banquet.'"
>
> (Luke 14:16-24)

Invited guests fail to fulfill a promise, offer excuses which demonstrate poor planning, have problems with priorities, miss the opportunity for joyful participation.

The host experiences rejection by those he counted upon, his effort and expenditure are not appreciated, he expresses resentment.

> *Four Soils.* "A farmer went out to sow his seed. As he was scattering the seed, some fell along the path, and the birds came and ate it up. Some fell on rocky places, where it did not have much soil. It sprang up quickly, because the soil was shallow. But when the sun came up, the plants were scorched, and they withered because

they had no root. Other seed fell among thorns, which grew up and choked the plants. Still other seed fell on a good soil, where it produced a crop – a hundred, sixty or thirty times what was sown. He who has ears, let him hear."

(Matthew 13:3-9)

Efforts to influence have varying results; responsiveness to input may be totally lacking, temporary, shoved aside by other concerns or well received.

Growth may be hindered by competing factors, difficulty in withstanding challenges, or failure to maintain a sense of priorities.

Good Samaritan. "A man was going down from Jerusalem to Jericho, when he fell into the hands of robbers. They stripped him of his clothes, beat him and went away, leaving him half dead. A priest happened to be going down the same road, and when he saw the man, he passed by on the other side. So too, a Levite, when he came to the place and saw him, passed by on the other side. But a Samaritan, as he traveled, came where the man was; and when he saw him, he took pity on him. He went to him and bandaged his wounds, pouring on oil and wine. Then he put the man on his own donkey, took him to an inn and took care of him. The next day he took out two silver coins and gave them to the innkeeper. 'Look after him,' he said, 'and when I return, I will reimburse you for any extra expense you may have.' Which of these three do you think was a neighbor to the man who fell into the hands of robbers?"

(Luke 10:30-36)

Compassionate help is given to a person who is hurting.

The hurting person may have "brought on his own problem" through poor judgment, yet he received aid.

Faith must find expression in action rather than appearance.

Helping may involve personal sacrifice.

Unappreciative Servant. "The kingdom of heaven is like a king who wanted to settle accounts with his servants. As he began the settlement, a man who owed him ten thousand talents was brought to him. Since he was not able to pay, the master ordered that he and his wife and his children and all that he had be sold to repay the debt. The servant fell on his knees before him. 'Be patient with me,' he begged, 'and I will pay back everything.' The servant's master took pity on him, canceled the debt and let him go. But when that servant went out, he found one of his fellow servants who owed him a hundred denarii. He grabbed him and began to choke him. 'Pay back what you owe me!' he demanded. His fellow servant fell to his knees and begged him, 'Be patient with me, and I will pay you back.' But he refused. Instead, he went off and had the man thrown into prison until he could pay the debt. When the other servants saw what had happened, they were greatly distressed and went and told their master everything that had happened. Then the master called the servant in. 'You wicked servant,' he said, 'I canceled all that debt of yours because you begged me to. Shouldn't you have had mercy on your fellow servant just as I had on you?' In anger his master turned him over to the jailers to be tortured, until he should pay back all he owed. This is how my heavenly Father will treat each of you unless you forgive your brother from your heart."

(Matthew 18:23-35)

A man requests patience with his own indebtedness, yet he is impatient with his fellow servant (double standard).

Difficulties may occur in both receiving and granting forgiveness.

Egocentrism of being forgiven of much, while not having a forgiving spirit toward others.

Rich fool. "The ground of a certain rich man produced a good crop. He thought to himself, 'What shall I do? I have no place to store my crops.' Then he said, 'This is what I'll do. I will tear down my barns and build bigger ones, and there I will store all my grain and my goods. And I'll say to myself, "You have plenty of good things laid up for may years. Take life easy; eat, drink and be merry."' But God said to him, 'You fool! This very night your life will be demanded from you. Then who will get what you have prepared for yourself?' This is how it will be with anyone who stores up things for himself but is not rich toward God."

(Luke 12:16-21)

A man shows regard only for the present, with no thought for eternal values.

He is *self*-centered – thinking to him*self*, talking to him*self*, considering only him*self*. In six sentences he says "I" six times, "my" five times, and "self" twice.

Obviously, counselors regularly work with people who have made poor choices, feel shame, struggle with forgiveness and forgiving, have problems in expressing anger, experience challenges of reconciliation, struggle with priorities, deal with family alienation, and suffer the negative effects of self-centeredness.

Another way to consider the relationships between Jesus' teachings and contemporary counseling challenges is to identify key issues which Christian counselors often encounter, then note metaphors in the gospels that speak to the issues. Some examples of this approach are shown in Table 1, with specific Scripture references detailed in the Appendix.

Table 1
Some Counseling Issues Addressed in Jesus' Metaphors

<u>Issue</u>	<u>Metaphors</u>
Sense of Identity	Salt of the earth, light of the world, branch connected to vine, sheep, fishers of men, child of God.
Self-examination	Clean cup, log in eye, prodigal son, eye is the lamp of the body.
Congruence	Yes-no sons, clean cup, unproductive fig tree, divided house, known by our fruits, whitewashed tombs.
Humility, Contentment	Choice of seats, inviting the lowly, prayer of the Pharisee, laborers in the vineyard.
Being Loved	Shepherd's search, prodigal son, lost coin, hen gathers chicks.
Growth, Change	Wine skins, patch on garment, seeds, leaven, unfruitful tree, four soils.
Use of Resources	Building a tower, waging a war, ten virgins, management of talents.
Wise Judgment	Faithful servant, shrewd steward, rich fool, prodigal son.
Priorities	Treasure in field, valuable pearl, four soils, good Samaritan, great banquet, pearls for pigs.
Anxiety, Worry	Birds of the air, lilies of the field.
Forgiveness	Prodigal son, money lender, unappreciative servant.
Restoring Relationships	Prodigal son, branch connected to the vine.
Self-centeredness	Rich fool, shrewd steward, good Samaritan, inviting the lowly,

	unappreciative servant, wedding feast, prayer of the Pharisee.
Social Interest	Good Samaritan, needy friend, rich man and Lazarus, feed sheep, inviting the lowly.

In light of the material cited from both the Old Testament and the New Testament, it is clear that the use of indirect communication did not originate with psychotherapists. Well before the contributions of Freud or Erickson there were many examples of the use of metaphor to "let the truth be learned by appearing not to teach."

Chapter 3

Metaphoric Stories in Christian Counseling

U se of metaphor in counseling is not considered to be a new school of thought, or an approach that would be used exclusively. As discussed in Chapter 1, parallel communication and purposeful stories are techniques which may be incorporated into the helper's usual interaction with the helpee to develop a therapeutic relationship, facilitate understanding, bypass defensiveness, allow the expression of salient feelings, recognize spiritual dimensions, and move to more effective functioning. Multilevel approaches may be utilized whether the basic theoretical orientation is dynamic, cognitive, relational, behavioral or existential. The Christian counselor may be in an advantageous position to use a metaphoric approach, given the precedence found in the Old Testament and the example set by Jesus in the gospels. We will now consider the development and delivery of stories designed to therapeutically influence the counselee.

Formulation of Stories

There are several basic principles involved in the formulation of metaphoric stories in a counseling setting.

1. Study the examples of acknowledged experts in counseling such as Barker (1985, 1996), Combs & Freedman (1990), Gordon (1978), Haley (1973, 1976), Lankton (1990), O'Hanlon (1987), Rosen (1982), Rossi & Ryan (1985), Siegelman (1990), Simpkins & Simpkins (2001), Zeig (1985), Zeig & Geary (2000), and Zeig & Gilligan (1990). Stories cited in Chapter 1 were drawn from some of these sources.

2. Become familiar with the numerous Scriptural examples of parallel communication and stories. Similes and analogies are abundant in the Psalms and Proverbs, many of which are specified in Chapter 2. Carefully review the parables told by Jesus, especially those having themes and characters that are likely to be relevant to counseling situations (see chart on page 32). Commentaries useful in understanding the parables told by Jesus include Barclay (1976a, b, c), Crossan (1975), Donahue (1990), Keener (1993), McFague (1975), Osborne (1991), and Scott (1990).

3. Be alert to current examples of themes addressed in Jesus' parables, especially those which would be related to counseling concerns. Jordan (1969) presents unique up-dates in his "cotton patch" approach. For example, the passage in Matthew 7:16-20 is translated as follows (p. 32):

A cultivated tree doesn't bear wild fruit, nor does a wild tree bear cultivated fruit. So, each tree may be known by the kind of fruit it produces. Also, people don't pick peaches from briars or grapes from a haw bush. A good man, from the good things stored in his heart, produces the good deed, while the mean person, from the mean things stored in his heart, produces the mean act. For the tongue is powered by the overflow from the heart. (cf. *Known by our fruits*)

Other examples of themes similar to those in Jesus' parables are found regularly in current news stories.

> Joey Levick, a 20-year-old man from the Seattle area, was out partying with two friends. For reasons that are not clear, the two young men turned against Joey and beat him severely. They broke his jaw, several ribs and two neck bones as they kicked him repeatedly with steel-toed boots. They left him in a ditch and fled. One went to his brother's house where he was able to clean up and get fresh clothes. He and his brother returned to the scene of the fight in order to retrieve cash and credit cards so that he could leave the state. Both men saw Joey sitting motionless by the ditch. This young man again saw Joey alive as he drove past the area on his way to Idaho.
>
> The second man also returned to the ditch with a friend. They saw Joey reach toward them with his hand. They left the scene. Later that evening, 16 hours after the fight, Joey was found dead. (cf. *Good Samaritan*)
>
> In 1935 a magnificent, streamlined ferry, which could carry 2000 passengers and 100 automobiles, began service in Seattle. The Kalakala was considered to be the finest art-deco sculpture ever crafted. For more than thirty years she served the Puget Sound area with regular daily routes, evening dance cruises, and weekend excursions to Victoria, B.C. After being retired from service in 1967, the Kalakala was taken to Alaska for use in crab processing. In the mid-1970's she was situated on a shore bed in Gibson Bay and used as a shrimp processing facility. Naturally, her structure and stature were severely compromised. In 1995, sixty years after the initial launching, some people in Seattle began a project to return and restore the

Kalakala. Much effort and investment were required to prepare her for the long voyage back to Seattle. Amid much ado, the great vessel was towed into Elliott Bay in 1998. Sponsors envisioned the day when the Kalakala would once again cruise the waters of Puget Sound, or perhaps become a tourist attraction as a conference center or a unique site for shops.

Alas, the Kalakala is still docked at the North end of Lake Union. Sponsors are having difficulty in keeping up on the monthly moorage costs, and no one has stepped forward to provide financing needed for the restoration. Whether the Kalakala will ever again be admired and enjoyed remains in doubt. Someone didn't count the cost. (cf. *Building a tower, waging a war*).

4.   Reflect upon your own experiences for stories relevant to needs of counselees. I have used the story of *Rafer* in working with clients who are struggling to overcome significant problems in childhood; whether physical, economic, racial or family difficulties.

I grew up in a small, predominately Swedish community in Central California. During the early 1950's there was one Black family in town. They were quite poor, living for a time in an abandoned boxcar. The children had an alcoholic father who had difficulty keeping a job, and a God-fearing mother who worked to make the best of the family's difficult circumstances. One day one of the little boys was terribly injured while playing in the nearby cannery. He nearly lost his leg. Though the leg was saved, the prognosis was bleak. He would probably always have a serious limp, and be limited in his ability to run and play with the other children.

When I was in junior high school, this same boy was a starter on the high school football and basketball teams, and he was an excellent track and field contender. He seemed to have overcome his limitations. Later he became the world decathlon champion ("the world's greatest all-round athlete"), the first Black person to be elected student body president at a major university (UCLA), and a significant figure in the development of the Special Olympics program ... Rafer Johnson.

In helping those with long-standing negative self-perceptions, I have found the *Spinach* story to be useful.

One day when I was in first grade, the cafeteria lunch included a glob of green and stringy gunk. It looked bad, smelled bad and tasted bad. As I returned my otherwise cleaned plate to the kitchen window, the well-meaning teacher on duty suggested that I should eat the rest of the "so-called" food. I resisted; she insisted. I resisted; she persisted. About ten minutes after I grudgingly complied, I became quite ill – losing all my lunch, even the good stuff! I interpreted my reaction as evidence of being seriously allergic to spinach. Throughout elementary school, junior high, college and graduate school I thought of myself as being allergic to spinach. There was never any doubt in my mind. Then, while in my early 30's, I attended a dinner party at which a green salad was served that contained odd-colored "lettuce." It was delicious! I complimented the hostess, only to find out that it was spinach salad. A short time later I enjoyed a tasty lasagna which I learned contained spinach. In neither situation did I experience nausea or any other uncomfortable reaction. I discovered that I was not allergic to spinach. For many, many years I had believed something about myself that was simply not true.

5. Attend to the metaphorical language used by counselees. Some examples have been mentioned (e.g., the woman who felt "crushed like a peanut", the man who thought he was Jesus). One of my clients described being paralyzed, and another person spoke of his early family experience as being on a "desolate island." Voth (1970) has observed that during periods of emotional intensity counselees may introduce metaphors that differ from their usual style, so attention to such differences may be useful. Milton Erickson made a therapeutic connection with a farm worker by talking about farm machinery.

Erickson was attempting to get Harold to take better care of himself, to eat more appropriately, to move out of his rundown shack and into better quarters. Harold was reluctant to follow this advice until Erickson started talking about how a tractor was only a machine meant to do farm work. Harold readily understood this analogy. Erickson pointed out that a farm machine should be properly cared for or it ceased being useful. He told Harold in great detail what the proper care of farm machinery involved. With this new framework Harold was willing to make the changes Erickson suggested in his hygiene and his living conditions.

(Haley, 1973, p. 128)

6. Note the ways in which counselees describe their experiences in terms of sensorial metaphors, then match the helping language to the dominant "representational system" (Brammer & MacDonald, 1999, p. 91, Gordon, 1978, p. 90). For example, a counselee may be primarily visual ("I see what you mean."), auditory ("I hear where you're coming from."), tactile ("That's very touching."), or kinesthetic ("That idea really grabs me"). The counselor may utilize language that reflects awareness of the favored sensory modality. A visually oriented person

may progress in the counseling program to the point of understanding that "the light at the end of the tunnel" is *daylight* rather than a *headlight*.

7. Formulate a story that is "isomorphic" – the characters and events that occur in the story are structurally equivalent to the counselee's situation (Barker, 1996, pp. 95-100; Gordon, 1978, pp. 19-26, 40-43). Thus, the people and the relationships in the metaphor are representative of the counselee's life situation, thereby enhancing the likelihood of successfully influencing the receiver. For instance, the parable of the *Prodigal Son* involves a father and two sons, with differing dynamics being experienced in each of the respective dyads. The *Spinach* story (page 39) involves an individual's interaction with an authority figure, then the development of an erroneous self-perception. Story selection and differential emphasis on players and roles are determined by the real-life situation of the counselee.

8. Be sensitive to new metaphors associated with advances in technology. "Surfing" is no longer an activity undertaken only by people at the beach; a "monitor" is something other than a supervisor in the halls of a school; a "mouse" is not just a pesky rodent. Developments in television, computers and other media provide rich sources for contemporary metaphor (Gozzi, 1999). Perhaps the basic idea of the "Vine and branches" metaphor could be conveyed as "Hub and stations" or "Windows and users".

Here is an example of a computer-related metaphor, used with a lady who had been having a secret affair with a married man who lived in the same apartment complex as she. Janet worked with computers regularly at her place of employment.

The other day I had a problem with my computer. It seems that a virulent virus infected my program. Although it got into the system in a rather limited, innocuous way, it was contagious and malignant.

We were very concerned about the impact it had on my programs, as well as the negative effects on other computers in the network. It was necessary to isolate the problematic computer and to work hard to inoculate against new attacks.

After hearing the *Computer* story, Janet became more open to the idea that her "secret" sin was notably affecting other aspects of her life, as well as other people.

9. Identify stories that involve animals in human-life activities. Some fairly tales may be appropriate, especially those which develop a good moral. I have worked with several people who were overly self-conscious or too self-centered, needing to hear the *Centipede* story.

A centipede was happy quite until a frog in fun said, "Pray, which leg comes after which?" Which raised her mind to such a pitch she fell distracted in a ditch considering how to run.

(Craster, 1937, p.155)

For those who are too anxious to take matters into their own hands or are impatient with God's timing and methods, the *Cocoon* story may be appropriate.

A man found a cocoon of a butterfly. One day a small opening appeared. He sat and watched the butterfly for several hours as it struggled to force its body through that little hole. Then it seemed to stop making any progress. It appeared as if it had gotten as far as it could, and it could go no farther.

Then the man decided to help the butterfly, so he took a pair of scissors and snipped off the remaining bit of the cocoon. The butterfly then emerged easily, but it had a swollen body and small, shriveled wings. The man continued to watch the butterfly because he expected that, at any moment, the wings would enlarge and expand to be able to support the body, which would contract in time. Neither happened!

The butterfly spent the rest of its life crawling around with a swollen body and shriveled wings. *It never was able to fly.* What the man did not understand in his kindness and haste was that the restricting cocoon and the struggle required for the butterfly to get through the tiny opening were God's way of forcing fluid from the body of the butterfly into its wings so that it would be ready for flight once it achieved its freedom from the cocoon. (Author unknown).

10. Appreciate the abundance of metaphor material in literature, myths and music. Christian music contains a wealth of similes and picturesque terms. Key words or phrases might be drawn from hymns or praise choruses (according to the age of the counselee!). For example, themes especially meaningful to counselees may include God the *great physician* (healer of the broken hearted), the *rock* (provider of secure refuge), or the *mighty fortress* (protector of the week and struggling); or Jesus as the *shepherd* (protective caregiver) or *friend* (sensitive helper). McMullin, in adapting his therapeutic approach to the culture of the Big Island of Hawaii, found that he needed to communicate with a "talking story" such as *The Cove of Black Pearls* (2000, p.418).

Delivery of Stories with Therapeutic Intent

Effective counseling involves the establishment of a therapeutic relationship between counselor and counselee. The process of developing such a relationship will typically include an understanding of past and current problems, perspectives on self and others, values, spiritual status, and strengths and weaknesses (i.e., getting into the counselee's "frame of reference"). At some point, especially in a brief therapy model, the counselor may decide to deliver a story or other metaphor in order to suggest ideas ("embed a thought"), reframe, or facilitate new patterns of thought. Such an approach may be especially useful if the counselee is rather resistant or in denial. Having identified an issue to be addressed, the counselor offers a well-formulated, goal-oriented story in a timely manner.

Scriptural examples and Ericksonian stories suggest several features of an effective metaphor. Stories told with the goal of influencing the hearer are *empathic, engaging, earthy, efficient*, and may have an *enigmatic ending.*

Empathic. When Jotham related the story about the trees selecting a king (Judges 9:8-15), the people were gathered beside the "great tree" preparing to crown Abimelech king. He got into the "frame of reference" of the listeners. Jesus was washing the feet of His disciples when He made the distinction between physical and spiritual cleanliness (John 13:10-11). In Chapter 2 we considered an analyst who used the idea of "mending the situation" as he worked with a tailor's son (Siegelman, 1990, p. 104). In each of these examples, sensitivity to the context provided the setting for a purposeful story. We Christian counselors use different metaphoric stories with those who are highly involved with sports (e.g., running the race, self-discipline) than those who are intrigued by crafts or interior design (e.g., counting the cost, part-whole relationships). In my work with a 35 year-old man who was struggling with homosexuality we were able to use our shared interest and experience in tennis to talk about how a tennis player would go about eliminating some unfortunate, self-defeating habits and move toward establishing more effective habits ... in *tennis* (e.g., identifying the difficulties, determining the desired grip and stance, focusing on proper form rather than simply discontinuing the problematic form, understanding that brief lapses are not indicative of failure or a need to stop trying to do better ... in *tennis*). The metaphoric approach helped the counselee develop a new, more hopeful perspective on his struggles relating to moving toward a desired change in sexual orientation.

<u>Engaging</u>. As Nathan confronted David about the issues of murder and adultery, he developed a sense of compassionate outrage as the wealthy man takes advantage of the poor man and kills the innocent little ewe lamb (II Samuel 12:1-7). Parables such as the *Good Samaritan* and the *Prodigal Son* involve dramatic, emotionally charged scenes. Jesus often included unexpected "twists" in His stories (e.g., the sudden death of the *Rich Fool,* the surprising inclusion of the poor and crippled from the streets at the *Great Banquet*). While counseling women who were sexually abused during childhood, I have used the following story to help prepare for the anticipated pain of bringing to awareness the hurt and anger that has been repressed for many years.

> When I was in college I accidentally collided with a sliding glass door while at a church-sponsored New Year's Eve party. (All of us were sober, I promise!) I incurred a rather deep cut on my right hand, requiring several stitches. (I show the scar to the counselee.) Contrary to the doctor's advice to rest the hand for a few days, I joined the group going to the Rose Parade the next day and resumed a fairly normal schedule of activities during the following days. The wound appeared to be healing adequately (the surface skin was gradually knitting back together), but there continued to be a deep throbbing and pain. Infection had set in! The only solution was to "irrigate" the wound which required that the injured area be re-opened and flushed out. It was a very uncomfortable procedure, but necessary for the full recovery process to begin. Only after the harmful and painful infection was cleared was I able to experience the inner healing.

The presentation of the *wounded hand* story may include humor, resistance to doctor's orders, and the irony of having to experience further pain in order to allow the healing process to begin.

Earthy. We learn from the Master Teacher the value of using well-known images from everyday life. Of course, the parable of the four soils is the epitome of an "earthy" story (pardon the pun), but more generally a well-formulated metaphor involves images and concepts that are quite familiar to the counselee. Several of the therapeutic stories that have been presented illustrate this guideline: The boy with and adopted dog (page 14), a married couple sharing a nice dinner (page 16), Harold's tractor (page 40), and the problematic computer (page 41).

Efficient. In both the Old Testament and the New Testament, purposeful stories were rather brief and simple. Verbalizing each of the Biblical stories would likely require no more than a minute or two. Similarly, the therapeutic stories in the literature, as well as the personal examples I have described, are relatively brief. Stories told to influence others, whether in the Bible or in the clinic, are also rather simple. There is usually only one basic point which is being conveyed, and the characters or situations are well known. For example, the *Rafer* story (page.38) may be told in less than two minutes, and the simple principle of overcoming significant problems experienced in childhood is readily understood.

Enigmatic Ending. Some of Jesus' parables ended in a rather obscure, open-ended manner. The story of the *Prodigal Son* ends without the family conflicts being resolved. The outcome of some parables included the element of surprise (e.g., the disdained Samaritan became the hero; the master praised the shrewd, unrighteous servant; the forgiven, freed servant who failed to be forgiving is sent to jail to be tortured). Some stories concluded with a perplexing question (e.g., "Which if these three proved to be a neighbor?"). The *Rich Fool* is asked about what will happen to the earthly treasures he had selfishly stored). In the same way, stories told in a counseling situation may end in a surprising, enigmatic, open-ended manner. For example, my *Spinach* story (page 39) ends with the sudden realization that I had a long-standing view of myself that was erroneous; the story of *Kalakala Ferry* (page 37) leaves the hearer uncertain as to the outcome.

In summary, there are numerous sources for developing therapeutic stories:

1. Study the examples of experts.
2. Examine the Scriptures for examples of metaphoric stories.
3. Note modern-day examples of themes addressed in Jesus' parables.
4. Reflect upon your own experience for stories relevant to needs of counselees.
5. Attend to the metaphors used by counselees.
6. Be sensitive to sensorial metaphors used by counselees.
7. Formulate stories that are isomorphic.
8. Watch for metaphors associated with advances in technology.
9. Identify meaningful stories that involve animals in human-like activity.
10. Appreciate the abundance of metaphor in literature, myth and music.

Effectively delivered stories with a purpose are empathic, engaging, earthy, efficient, and may have an enigmatic ending. Of course, any use of metaphor should be individualized, taking into account the history and current issues being addressed in therapy. For example, with Sally (an older lady with a long-standing history of very low self-esteem), I found the *Spinach* story (page 39) to be useful; for Sue (a 40 year old single lady who was physically and sexually abused in childhood), I found the story of *Rafer* (page 38) to be helpful as she struggled with overcoming long-standing emotional pain.

Chapter 4

Metaphoric Activities in Christian Counseling

Just as Ericksonian therapists may incorporate metaphoric activities into their work with counselees (cf, a married couple goes to dinner, page 16), Christian counselors may have occasion for incorporating a physical activity into the process of indirect communication. As found in the use of therapeutic stories, a metaphorically meaningful activity may be quite useful to make an important point or bypass resistance. Three examples are given to illustrate activities with therapeutic purpose.

I was working with a 40 year old, single woman who had been abused in various ways by several people during her childhood, and had been involved in some relationships as an adult for which she felt guilty. We had worked through both sets of problems emotionally and cognitively, and during the counseling process she publicly expressed her spiritual efforts of renewal. There had been much progress, yet we both sensed a need for further closure to some residual feelings with which she continued to struggle. At the end of a counseling session I gave her an assignment which involved metaphoric activities.

The counselee was asked to return to her home

and get out two sheets of blank paper. On one sheet she was to list the people who had hurt her, and toward whom she still had resentment, anger or disappointment. On the other sheet she was to briefly describe those situations for which she was continuing to feel guilt due to failure of self-forgiveness. She was to place both sheets in a paper bag and carry the container down to the local ferry. She was to board the ferry for the 30-minute ride across Puget Sound *without looking back* (just like the instructions to Lot's wife). After disembarking, counselee was to go down to the beach area and *pray* for God's help in getting rid of these noxious, residual feelings. Then she was to find a big, ugly bin and *throw away* the paper bag which contained her writings. She was asked to board the next ferry and return home *without looking back*, then go to a local restaurant near the landing and have a private celebration of what had just occurred.

The next morning at the office there was a phone message from the counselee thanking me for the assignment and indicating that she was feeling positive about the event. The feeling tone of subsequent counseling sessions indicted that much of the burden had been lifted.

Vernick (Vernick and Thurman, 2002) described his use of a metaphor with a woman who was struggling with self-image issues. She had always felt inferior to an older brother and was envious of his power and position in the family. She described herself as small and insignificant, and she resented her parents' affirmations of her brother, and believed, by comparison, that she was inadequate. We examined her untrue thoughts, yet what helped her feel differently about herself was a well-timed metaphor.

Over several weeks, I noticed that when we began our sessions, she often commented about the flower garden outside my office. With this in mind, I asked her if she'd like to see two sets of my favorite flowers. She agreed, so we went outside and I pointed to a bush filled with red roses. It was big, bold and dramatic. She was impressed, and I said, "Yes, it is lovely, but it could hurt you when you get too close to its thorns, and it requires a lot of upkeep in order to look so beautiful." But we agreed it was gorgeous and demanded to be noticed.

Off in a more secluded and shady spot was my other favorite, a beautifully delicate specimen, a bleeding heart. This small bush had tiny, paper-thin, heart-shaped pink flowers that dangled from their stems like a tear that's about to fall. I remarked, "The bleeding heart is a very different flower than the rose but equally as lovely." My client nodded silently. Then I asked her to think about something. "What if the bleeding heart thought it was not as beautiful or as important just because it was not big and showy like the rose? Do you suppose my garden would be as beautiful if all the flowers were roses?"

She began to cry and I knew that she received the truth behind the story. We then processed her feelings during the session, and a shift in her self-perception occurred. Greenberg and Korman (1993) suggest that when we fail to pick up on in-session affective experiences, we neglect a crucial element of bringing about therapeutic change in our clients' lives (pp. 376-377).

In working with a married couple, I found the *trust fall* to be a helpful technique.

After ten years of marriage, Sam had been unfaithful to Joan. He repented, discontinued the adulterous relationship, sought Joan's forgiveness, assured her that it would never happen again, and entered into counseling. The therapy included discussions relating to the issues of forgiveness, re-establishment of trust, and family dynamics.

At the verbal level, there appeared to be much gain, but further progress seemed to be blocked for unknown reasons. Suspecting that Joan was still struggling with her trust of Sam, I asked them to stand with me in the center of the counseling office and participate in an "experiment." After ruling out any back problems for Sam, I suggested that Joan stand about four feet in front of Sam, facing away from him. "Joan, do you believe that Sam would catch you if you were to 'let go' and fall backward?" "Yes." "Do you think that Sam would trick you and let you fall to the floor?" "No." "Joan, can you entrust yourself to Sam by falling back into his arms?" "Sure!" I then asked her to let herself fall backward and allow Sam to catch her. She tried to fall numerous times, but could not "let go" and entrust herself to him. I then replaced Sam in the catcher position, and Joan allowed herself to fall backward on the second try. As a result of this experiment, we were able to engage in deeper discussions of Joan's continuing distrust of her husband. At a later date, she was able to fall into Sam's arms, entrusting herself to him.

The guiding principle in using a metaphoric activity for therapeutic purposes is to "translate" a psychological issue into a physical expression. In the examples above the guilty woman left her hurt and shame behind, both literally and figuratively; the woman who felt inferior was able to more fully appreciate differing types of beauty (her own included); and Joan developed insight into her feelings, then entrusted herself (both physically and emotionally) to her husband. Christian counselors may consider the many Biblical examples of symbolic, metaphoric activities, then develop creative ways to help counselees by translating psychological issues into therapeutic actions.

Chapter 5

Practical Issues in the Use of Metaphor in Christian Counseling

As we consider the use of metaphor in Christian counseling, several questions emerge:

How often should metaphoric stories be used? Those engaging in long-term psychotherapy would advise limited use of stories due to the possibility of projections of the therapist and the potential impact on the transference (Siegelman, 1990); client-centered counselors may view indirect influence as too directive in a nondirective approach; and helpers using a strategic, brief-therapy model may use a well-designed story in most cases. There is no research that addresses the issue of frequency, so clinical judgment is to be used to determine how often to use a metaphoric approach.

What about interpretation of the metaphor? Most counselors follow the example of Jesus (knowingly or unknowingly) and do not usually interpret the story. Some Bible scholars believe that to interpret a parable is to destroy it as a parable, thereby losing the aesthetic dimension as well as its evocative power (Osborne, 1991, p.245). Milton Erickson was unwilling to interpret his stories for the counselee, feeling that the depth and swiftness of behavioral change could be prevented if the person "suffers a translation" of the communication (Haley, 1973, p.28). The general thought is that the metaphor will be understood at the level needed by the counselee. Gordon (1978) describes the rationale of *not* interpreting stories delivered with therapeutic intent.

> By refraining from specific interpretation we force the hearers to derive and employ their own interpretations of "what is really going on". Since the metaphor is for the client, only his rendering of it can be exactly correct. As the tailor, your job is to select the material and to properly cut out the pattern for the garment. It is the customer who does the alterations so that the garment fits (p.51).

Gafner and Benson (2003) never discuss a story's meaning immediately, thereby allowing the metaphorical story to "percolate" in the counselee's unconscious mind. They suggest that the individual meaning derived by the counselee may be discussed during the next session, giving further opportunity for the development of insight (p.8). Thus the counselor seeks to present a well-formulated and timely story with therapeutic intent, but the personalization and application is the responsibility of the counselee. An individual's response to metaphor will be greatly influenced by past experiences, psychological needs and world-view.

May a story be used with more than one counselee? Yes. Thompson (1990) suggests that the counselor may develop a repertoire of stories that can be applied to a variety of situations, with necessary adjustments of emphasis according to the circumstances unique to the individual being counseled (p.254). There may be several counselees that have somewhat similar key issues. I have used the *Spinach* story (see page 39) in several situations that involved long-standing low self-esteem. The story of *Rafer* (see page 38) may be used to highlight childhood difficulties related to physical or family or economic or racial issues. The *Prodigal Son* may be shared with the emphasis on the forgiving father, the repentant son or the jealous son. Each time a story is delivered there may be selected aspects of the account that are emphasized through the tone of voice, pauses or inflections. Of course, the emphasis chosen will be determined by the goals of therapy and the immediate needs of the counselee.

Should metaphor be used with all counselees? As would be true for most any therapeutic technique, a metaphoric approach is not effective for all counselees. Siegelman (1990, Ch.9) suggest that use of metaphor is contraindicated when the counselee is (1) rather concrete in thinking, taking everything too literally; (2) unable to engage in imaginative, creative thought; or (3) lacking in the ability to be playful. Obviously, those who are struggling with distinguishing between reality and fantasy (i.e., thought disorder) are not good candidates for the rather abstract, intuitive processes needed to appreciate parables or stories with therapeutic intent (Plaut, 1966).

What about seeding? When counselors anticipate delivering a parable or story with therapeutic intent, they may wish to "prepare the way" by alluding to the basic theme of the intervention prior to presenting the metaphor. This is termed *seeding* in Ericksonian literature (Haley, 1973; Gafner and Benson, 2003; Zeig, 1990), and is similar to the concept of priming in memory research or foreshadowing in literature. By making reference to an idea prior to its more complete development, the counselor seeks to create a more receptive mind-set in the counselee, thereby reducing resistance and facilitating the likelihood of good reception and utilization of the metaphor. For example, if I were to determine that the story of the *Prodigal Son* would be appropriate, I might allude to the idea of forgiveness two or three times before telling the parable. Similarly, if the *Spinach* story is to be presented, I make reference to the importance of self-concept in mental health. Care must be given lest we overdo the seeding (Gafner and Benson, 2003).

The use of indirect communication has value for Christian counselors. There is precedent in both Scripture and professional literature for the use of metaphor to understand and positively influence those we teach or counsel. In order to effectively use the skills which have been described, we will need to *practice* thinking metaphorically, *practice* translating counseling issues into material for stories, and *practice* engaging in parallel communication. It will be necessary for us to become observant, noting the processes of nature and the activities of people in our community; use our abilities to understand people and communicate well with them, sometimes indirectly; encourage those with whom we work to make significant changes in their thinking, feeling, and relationship with God and others. We can become more like the man who grew up in a carpenter's home.

> *A word aptly spoken is like*
> *apples of gold in settings of silver.*
>
> *(Proverbs 25:11)*

References

Barclay, W. (1976a). *The gospel of John* (Rev. ed.). Philadelphia: Westminster Press.

Barclay, W. (1976b). *The gospel of Luke* (Rev. ed.). Philadelphia: Westminster Press.

Barclay, W. (1976c). *The gospel of Matthew* (Rev. ed.). Philadelphia: Westminster Press.

Barker, P. (1985). *Using metaphors in psychotherapy.* New York: Brunner/Mazel.

Barker, P. (1996). *Psychotherapeutic metaphors: A guide to theory and practice.* New York: Brunner/Mazel.

Blessing, K. (2002). The "Confusion Technique" of Milton Erickson as hermeneutic for

Biblical parables. *Journal of Psychology and Christianity, 21,* 161-168.

Brammer, L.M. & MacDonald, G.M. (1999). *The helping relationship: Process and skills.* (7th ed.), Boston: Allyn and Bacon.

Combs, G. & Freedman, J. (1990). *Symbol, story and ceremony: Using metaphor in individual and family therapy.* New York: Norton.

Craster, E. (1937). The puzzled centipede. In Brewton, J.E. (Ed.), *Under the tent in the sky.* New York: MacMillan.

Crossan, J.D. (1975). *The dark interval: Towards a theology of story.* Allen, TX: Argus Communications.

Donahue, J. R. (1990). *The gospel in parable.* Minneapolis: Fortress Press.

Gafner, G., & Benson, S. (2003). *Hypnotic techniques.* New York: Norton.

Gilligan, S.G. (1990). *Coevolution of primary process in brief therapy.* In Zeig, J.K. & Gilligan, S.G. (Eds), *Brief therapy: Myths methods, and metaphors.* New York: Brunner/Mazel.

Gordon, D. (1978). *Therapeutic metaphors: Helping others through the looking glass.* Cupertino, CA: Meta.

Gozzi, R. (1999). *The power of metaphor in the age of electronic media.*

Cresskill, N.J.:Hampton Press.

Greenberg, L. S., & Korman, L. (1993). Assimilating emotion into psychotherapy integration. *Journal of Psychotherapy Integration, 3,* 249-265.

Haley, J. (1973). *Uncommon Therapy: The psychiatric techniques of Milton H. Erickson, M.D.* New York: Norton.

Haley, J. (1976). *Problem – solving therapy.* New York: Harper & Row.

Ingram, D. H. (1996). The vigor of metaphor in clinical practice. *The American Journal of Psychoanalysis,* 56(1), 17-34

Jordan, C. (1969). *Cotton patch version of Luke and Acts.* New York: Association Press.

Keener, C.S. (1993). *The IVP Bible background commentary: New Testament.* Downers Grove, Il.: Intervarsity Press.

Kopp, S. (1971). *Guru: Metaphors for a psychotherapist.* Palo Alto, CA: Science and Behavior Books.

Lankton, S. (1990). *The broader implications of Ericksonian therapy.* New York: Ericksonian Monographs.

McFague, S. (1975). *Speaking in parables: A study in metaphor and theology.* Philadelphia: Fortress Press.

McMullin, R.E. (2000). *The new handbook of cognitive therapy techniques.* New York: Norton.

Madanes, C. (1990). Strategies and metaphors in brief therapy. In Zeig, J.K. & Gilligan, S.G. (Eds), *Brief Therapy: Myths, methods, and metaphors.* New York: Brunner/Mazel.

O'Hanlon, W.H. (1987). *Taproots: Underlying principles of Milton Erickson's Therapy and Hypnosis.* New York: Norton.

Osborne, G.R. (1991). *The hermeneutical spiral.* Downers Grove, Il: Intervarsity Press.

Plaut, A. (1966). Reflections about not being able to imagine. *Journal of Analytical Psychology, 11,* 113-133.

Rosen, S. (1982). *My voice will go with you.* New York: Norton

Rossi, E. & Ryan, M. (Eds.). (1985). *Life reframing in hypnosis: The seminars, works and lectures of Milton H. Erickson.* New York: Irvington.

Scott, B.B. (1990). *Hear then the parable.* Minneapolis: Fortress Press.

Sieglman, E.Y. (1990). *Metaphor and meaning in psychotherapy.* New York: Guilford Press.

Simpkins, C.A. & Simpkins, A.M. (2001). *Timeless Teaching from the Therapy Masters.* San Diego: Radiant Dolphin Press.

Thompson, K.F. (1990). Metaphor: A Myth with a Method. In Zeig, J.K. & Gilligan, S.G. (Eds.), *Brief Therapy: Myths, Methods, and Metaphors.* New York: Brunner/Mazel.

Vernick, L. & Thurman, C. (2002). Change in process. In Clinton, T. & Ohlschalger, G., *Competent Christian Counseling.* Colorado Springs: Waterbrook Press.

Victor, G. (1977). Interpretations couched in mystical imagery. In Siegelman, E.Y., *Metaphor and meaning in psychotherapy.* New York: Guilford Press.

Voth, H. (1970). The analysis of metaphor. *Journal of the American Psychoanalytic Association, 18,* 599-621

Zeig, J.K. (1985). *Experiencing Erickson: An introduction to the man and his work.* New York: Brunner/Mazel.

Zeig, J.K. (1990) Seeding. In Zeig, J.K. & Gilligan, S.G. (Eds), *Brief Therapy: Myths, Methods, and Metaphors.* New York: Brunner/Mazel.

Zeig, J.K. & Geary, B.D. (Eds.). (2000). *The Letters of Milton Erickson.* Phoenix: Zeig, Tucker & Theisen, Inc.

Zeig, J.K. & Gilligan, S.G. (1990). *Brief therapy: Myths, Methods and Metaphors.* New York: Brunner/Mazel.

Appendix

Metaphor	Reference
Birds of the air	Matthew 6:26
Branch connected to vine	John 15:1-8
Building a tower	Luke 14:28-30
Child of God	Matthew 7:11, 18:3-4; Ephesians 5:1
Choice of seats	Luke 14:8-11, 20:45-47
Clean cup	Matthew 23:25-26
Divided house	Matthew 12:25
Eye is the lamp	Matthew 6:22-23
Faithful servant	Matthew 24:45-51; Mark 13:33-37; Luke 12:42-46
Feed sheep	John 21:15-17
Fishers of men	Matthew 4:19; Luke 1:17
Four soils	Matthew 13:3-9; Mark 4:3-8; Luke8: 5-8
Good Samaritan	Luke 10:30-37
Great Banquet	Matthew 22:1-14; Luke 14:16 24
Hen gathers chicks	Matthew 23:37
Inviting the lowly	Luke 14:12-14
Known by our fruits	Matthew 7:15-20; Luke 6:43-45
Laborers in vineyard	Matthew 20:1-16

__Metaphor__	__Reference__
Leaven	Matthew 13:3; Luke 13:20-21
Light of the world	Matthew 5:14-16
Lilies of the field	Matthew 6:28-29
Log in eye	Matthew 7:3-5; Luke 6:41-42
Lost coin	Luke 15:8-10
Management of talents	Matthew 25:14-30; Luke 19:11-27
Money lender	Luke 7:41-43
Needy friend	Luke 11:5-10
Patch on garment	Matthew 9:16; Mark 2:21; Luke 5:36
Pearls for pigs	Matthew 7:6
Prayer of Pharisee	Matthew 7:6; Luke 18:10-14
Prodigal Son	Luke 15:11-32
Rich fool	Luke 12:13-21
Rich man and Lazarus	Luke 16:19-31
Salt of the earth	Matthew 5:13
Seeds	Matthew 13:3-9,31-32; Mark 4:3-8, 30-32; Luke 8:5-8, 13:18-19
Sheep	John 10:1-18
Shepherd's search	Matthew 18:12-14; Luke 15:4-7
Shrewd steward	Luke 16:1-8
Ten virgins	Matthew 25:1-13
Treasure in field	Matthew 13:44
Unfruitful tree	Matthew 7:19, 21:18-22; Luke 13:6-9
Unappreciative servant	Matthew 18:23-35
Valuable pearl	Matthew 13:45
Waging war	Luke 14:31-33
Whitewashed tombs	Matthew 23:27-28; Luke 11:44
Wineskins	Matthew 9:17; Mark 2:22; Luke 5:37-38
Yes-No sons	Matthew 21:28-32

Name Index

Index of Metaphoric Stories and Activities

Subject Index

Printed in the United States
15697LVS00001B/22-24